My
Family
History

by Nancy Burgeson

Illustrations by Aija Janums

Troll Associates

Library of Congress Cataloging-in-Publication Data

Burgeson, Nancy.
   My family history / by Nancy Burgeson; illustrated by Aija
Janums.
      p.   cm.—(A Troll family guide)
   Summary: A handbook for tracing your family roots and recording
your family history.
   ISBN 0-8167-2794-5 (pbk.)
   1. Genealogy—Juvenile literature.   2. United States—Genealogy—
Handbooks, manuals, etc.—Juvenile literature.   3. Oral history—
Juvenile literature.   [1. Genealogy—Handbooks, manuals, etc.
2. Oral history—Handbooks, manuals, etc.]   I. Janums, Aija, ill.
II. Title.   III. Series.
CS16.B87   1993
929'.1—dc20   92-3086

Have you ever wondered what life was like before you were born? Or who your ancestors were? Have you heard your parents talk about your Great Aunt Minny and your cousin who was a famous circus performer? Who were these people and exactly how are they related to you?

Use this book to trace your roots and learn about your heritage! Fill it in as you please. Some pages have room for special additions, like photographs and clippings. You can even start a family tree. *So get going....* Use this book to unlock the past! It could be one of the most exciting adventures of your life!

Start a family tree! It doesn't have to be complicated. You may only want to list names, dates and places of birth. Start with yourself and work backwards through your parents, grandparents, great-grandparents, and so on. Try to write down facts for each generation until you discover who your earliest relatives were.

Fill in as much information as you know.

Your name _____

Place of birth _____

Date _____

Hometown _____

Other facts _____

Mother's name_____

Place of birth _____

Date _____

Hometown _____

Other facts _____

Father's name _____

Place of birth _____

Date _____

Hometown _____

Other facts _____

Grandmother's name _____

Place of birth _____

Date _____

Hometown _____

Other facts _____

Grandfather's name _____

Place of birth _____

Date _____

Hometown _____

Other facts _____

Grandmother's name _____

Place of birth _____

Date _____

Hometown _____

Other facts _____

Grandfather's name _____

Place of birth _____

Date _____

Hometown _____

Other facts _____

Great-grandmother's name _____

Place of birth _____

Date _____

Hometown _____

Other facts _____

Great-grandfather's name _____

Place of birth _____

Date _____

Hometown _____

Other facts _____

Great-grandmother's name _____

Place of birth _____

Date _____

Hometown _____

Other facts _____

Great-grandfather's name _____

Place of birth _____

Date _____

Hometown _____

Other facts _____

Great-grandmother's name _____

Place of birth _____

Date _____

Hometown _____

Other facts _____

Great-grandfather's name _____

Place of birth _____

Date _____

Hometown _____

Other facts _____

Great-grandmother's name _____

Place of birth _____

Date _____

Hometown _____

Other facts _____

Great-grandfather's name _____

Place of birth _____

Date _____

Hometown _____

Other facts _____

What Do You Know About YOU?

My name is _____

I live at _____

I'm _____ and in the _____ grade.
         age

I was born in _____
                              hospital

_____
         city   state

on _____
              month/day/year

The time was _____ I weighed _____

My zodiac sign is _____

I can speak _____ language(s):_____

_____

Injuries I have had: _____

_____

and other things like:_____

_____

I have a pet _____ whose name is

_____

The neatest thing my pet does is _____

_____

If I could call anyone in the world, I'd call _____

_____and say _____

_____

What I like most about school: _____

_____

What I like to do after school:_____

_____

What I like to do with my friends: _____

_____

This summer I want to _____

_____

The world record I would like to set is_____

_____

My predictions for the future are _____

_____

Pictures of ME.

ME as a baby!

ME this year!

My mother's name is _____

My father's name is _____

I have _____ brother(s).

I have _____ sister(s).

My sisters' and brothers' names are _____

_____

My parents' anniversary is _____

Things I like to do with my family: _____

_____

If I were my mother or father for a day, I would

_____

_____

_____

_____

_____

_____

_____

Record new information as it happens.

	NAME	DATE	CITY/STATE	COUNTRY
Births:				
Marriages:				
Deaths:				
Other events:				

Map

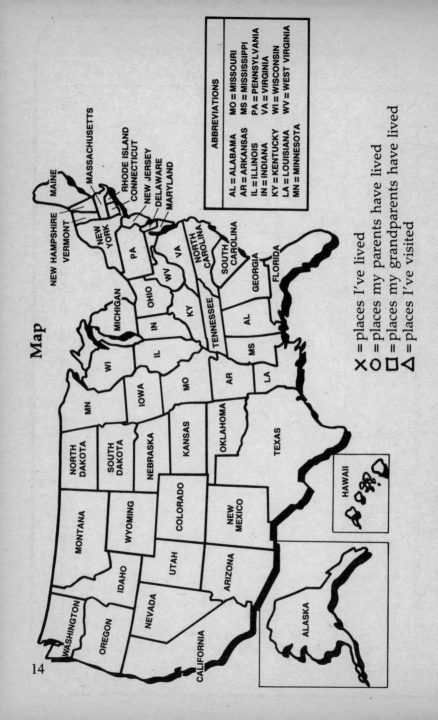

14

ABBREVIATIONS

AL = ALABAMA	MO = MISSOURI
AR = ARKANSAS	MS = MISSISSIPPI
IL = ILLINOIS	PA = PENNSYLVANIA
IN = INDIANA	VA = VIRGINIA
KY = KENTUCKY	WI = WISCONSIN
LA = LOUISIANA	WV = WEST VIRGINIA
MN = MINNESOTA	

X = places I've lived
O = places my parents have lived
□ = places my grandparents have lived
△ = places I've visited

Family Journey

The first relative(s) to come to this country:

_____

Arrived at _____
(location)

On _____
(date)

From _____
(place)

Came by _____
(transportation)

The journey took_____
(hours)

Memories:_____

_____

_____

First lived in: _____

Other places: _____

Languages spoken:_____

_____

_____

_____

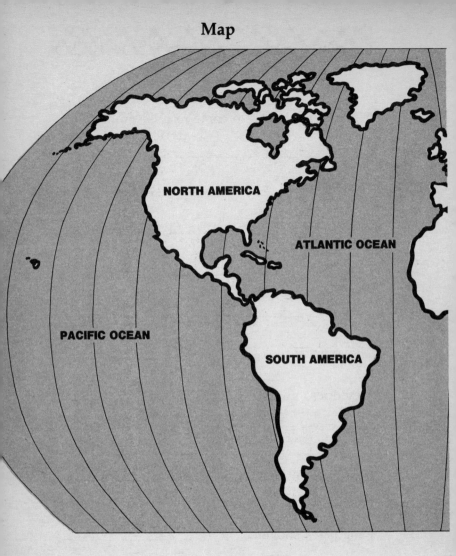

This map of the world shows where my ancestors came from and where they settled. The symbols in the key show how they traveled.

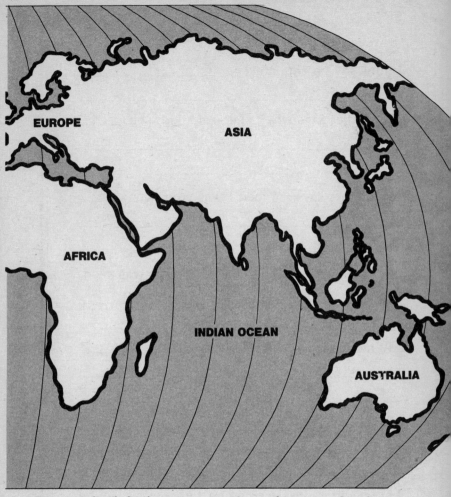

EUROPE

ASIA

AFRICA

INDIAN OCEAN

AUSTRALIA

For more detailed information, consult an atlas or encyclopedia.

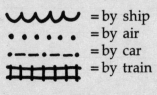

= by ship
= by air
= by car
= by train

The Generation Gap

I think my parents are _____
_____

My mother says when she was a kid, she _____
_____
_____

My mother says, "When I was your age, I_____
_____
_____

My grandparents say when my mother was a kid,
she _____
_____

My father says when he was a kid, he_____
_____
_____

My father says, "When I was your age, I _____
_____
_____

My grandparents say when my father was a kid, he
_____
_____
_____

CHECK IF YOU REMEMBER WHEN THERE WERE NO:

	You	Parents	Grandparents (Mother)	Grandparents (Father)	Other
color televisions					
refrigerators					
instant cameras					
pocket calculators					
radios					
skateboards					
space shuttles					
fast food stands					
shopping malls					
electric can openers					
juke boxes					
microwave ovens					
video games					
airplanes					
computers					

19

Love and Marriage

Where my parents met _____

How they met _____

_____

My mother was _____ and my father was _____
                  age   age

My parents went together for _____

They were married on _____ in _____
                       month/day/year   place

_____

What they remember about their wedding and their

first home: _____

_____

_____

_____

Paste photos or clippings here.

Where and how my mother's parents met _____

_____

_____

They were married on _____, in _____
                        date   city/state

_____

Where and how my father's parents met_____

_____

_____

They were married on _____, in _____
                        date   city/state

_____

Their memories: _____

_____

_____

_____

_____

_____

_____

_____

_____

_____

Family Record-Breakers

Who is the OLDEST?_____

Who is the YOUNGEST? _____

Who is the TALLEST? _____

Who is the SHORTEST? _____

Who is the FUNNIEST? _____

Who is the MOST FAMOUS? _____

Who is the BEST STORYTELLER? _____

Family Record-Holders

Anyone in the family who has...

Had twins?	name:
Been on television or radio?	name:
Been in the newspaper?	name:
Won any awards or prizes?	name:
Traveled around the world?	name:
Marched in a parade?	name:
Invented something special?	name:
Performed on the stage?	name:

ABC's

The schools I have attended _____

_____

_____

_____

The names of my favorite teachers _____

_____

_____

_____

Diplomas, honors, awards I received _____

_____

_____

_____

My mother's favorite teacher was _____

Her best subject was _____

My father's favorite teacher was_____

His best subject was _____

My grandparents' best subjects were _____

_____

_____

_____

Food

My favorite restaurant is _____

_____

My favorite meal consists of _____

_____

My mother's favorite meal is _____

_____

My father's favorite meal is _____

_____

My mother's favorite recipe is for _____

_____

_____

My father's favorite recipe is for_____

_____

_____

25

Family Traditions

How my family celebrates:

Birthdays _____

Weddings _____

Anniversaries _____

Graduations _____

Special family songs: _____

dances: _____

foods: _____

gifts: _____

Traditions that have been carried on in my family:

_____

_____

_____

_____

_____

_____

_____

_____

_____

_____

How my family celebrates:

New Year's Day	
Valentine's Day	
Easter	
Passover	
Memorial Day	
Fourth of July	
Labor Day	
Halloween	
Election Day	
Thanksgiving	
Christmas	
Chanukah	
Others:	

Whistle While You Work

Jobs I've had _____

_____

My allowance _____

_____

My mother's first job was_____

_____

How times have changed _____

_____

My father's first job was _____

_____

How times have changed _____

_____

My grandparents' first jobs were _____

_____

More comments: _____

_____

_____

_____

_____

_____

_____

_____

Family Ties

The parents of your father or mother are your grandparents.

The parents of your grandfather or grandmother are your great-grandparents.

The children of your brothers and sisters are your nephews and nieces, and you are their uncle or aunt.

Your parents' brothers and sisters are your uncles and aunts and you are their nephew or niece.

The children of your aunts and uncles are your cousins.

MY FAMILY HISTORY

_____

_____

_____

_____

_____

_____

_____

_____

_____

_____

_____

_____

_____

_____

_____

_____

_____

ME _____
BROTHERS and SISTERS
_____
_____

MOTHER
_____

FATHER
_____

GRANDPARENTS
_____
_____

GRANDPARENTS
_____
_____

GREAT-GRANDPARENTS
_____
_____

GREAT-GRANDPARENTS
_____
_____

_____
_____

_____
_____

31

Things You Can Do

Photograph relatives and friends, places, and events. Set aside a drawer, box, or old suitcase for family keepsakes.

Visit family historical landmarks. Save something special from the area, like a stone.

Write to chambers of commerce and visitors' bureaus for maps, historical descriptions, and general information about your ancestors' countries of origin.

Search old records for clues. Look for things written in old books. Sometimes old books were used to record births, marriages, and deaths in the family.

Start a family scrapbook.

Send copies of your family tree to relatives. Ask them to add information.

Make a poster-size family tree and include photos and clippings. Hang it in your room!